Climbing and Wall Plants

A Wisley Handbook

Climbing and Wall Plants

GEORGE PRESTON

Cassell

The Royal Horticultural Society

THE ROYAL HORTICULTURAL SOCIETY

Cassell Educational Limited
Wellington House
125 Strand
London WC2R 0BB
for the Royal Horticultural Society

First published 1973
Second edition 1986
Reprinted 1987, 1989
Third edition 1992
Reprinted 1995

British Library Cataloguing in Publication Data
A catalogue record for this book is available from the
British Library

ISBN 0-304-32032-3

Photographs by Pat Johns, George Preston, Martyn Rix,
Harry Smith Horticultural Collection, Michael Warren.

Phototypesetting by Chapterhouse Ltd, Formby
Printed in Hong Kong by Wing King Tong Co. Ltd

Cover: honeysuckle, roses and other plants tumble over a
mellow brick wall.
p. 1: *Lonicera japonica* 'Halliana', a twiner with
wonderfully fragrant flowers.
   Photographs by Eric Crichton Photos
p. 2: *Abutilon vitifolium* needs a sheltered, sunny position
to bloom from May to July.
Back cover: *Parthenocissus qinquefolia* in its autumn
colour and *Hedera colchica* 'Dentata Variegata'.
   Photograph by Andrew Lawson

Contents

	page
Introduction	7
Soil preparation and planting	9
Artificial support	12
Fan training	13
Espalier	13
Feeding	16
Pruning	17
Winter protection	19
Perennial climbing and wall plants	20
Annual climbing plants	53
Wall trained fruit	59
Some recommended varieties	61
Plants suitable for various aspects	63
A selection for north and east walls	63
A selection for a west wall	64
A selection for a south wall	64

Above: a mixture of annuals and perennials clothing a wall.
Below left: *Abutilon megapotamicum*, an evergreen shrub from Brazil for a sheltered corner (see p. 20). Below right: *Actinidia chinensis*, the Kiwi fruit, a vigorous climber, grown in particular for its handsome leaves (see p.20).

Introduction

Walls in a garden provide an opportunity for growing some special plants. Most walls provide shelter and so some extra warmth which may enable a plant to flourish in a district with a colder climate than its native country. For instance plants from the Mediterranean region will grow well in many parts of Britain against a south wall.

Climbing plants are those which have a natural means of supporting themselves, such as ivy (by its aerial roots), Boston ivy, often incorrectly called Virginia creeper (by its adhesive pads at the end of tendrils), honeysuckle (by its twining stems) or clematis (by its twining leaf stems).

The term is also used to cover many other plants which can be fixed to the wall artificially, for example tied in to a framework. Among these are the so-called climbing roses, which if grown in the open would make an untidy, sprawling bush like a blackberry, and also many less hardy shrubs which are trained against the wall, but which would make a bush or small tree if grown in the open.

Many of the climbing plants are indispensable to cover a large unsightly wall. Familiar examples are Boston ivy, *Parthenocissus*

Buddleja colvilei, a striking Himalayan species which needs some protection in winter for its first few years (see p. 21).

tricuspidata, which provides a wonderful display of colour just before leaf fall, or the various forms of ivy, *Hedera helix*. Ivies, being evergreen, are valuable in providing colour all year round, those with yellow or white leaf variegations being of particular value in the dull days of winter. It would, however, be a waste of a good opportunity to use only plants such as ivy to cover a wall; a varied selection of other ornamental plants will bring interest at different times of the year.

The walls of houses or boundary walls provide ideal positions for climbing and other plants, including fruit trees, but one must always estimate the vigour and size to which the plant will eventually grow before planting, and consider the possible effect on the house. In most cases it is undesirable to have climbers growing too high, for with these it is difficult to prune and tie in the new growth; they may grow over windows, obscuring the view into the garden, and into the roof gutters causing blockages. Plants with a very strong root system can damage the foundations of the house if planted against a wall. Therefore the selection of the most suitable type of plant for the right position is most important.

On the whole, climbers, especially the more vigorous ones, are not as satisfactory as shrubs for covering walls of moderate height. In many cases they have a strong tendency to climb to the top of the wall leaving the lower parts bare. However, they can sometimes be trained along the top of the wall, leaving the lower spaces for shrubs. As I have already said, the great value of walls is not in providing accommodation for climbers alone, but also in affording conditions that enable beautiful shrubs, which are tender in the open ground, to grow successfully.

A colourful combination of *Parthenocissus tricuspidata* and pyracantha.

Soil preparation and planting

For plants that are to be grown on boundary walls, no new soil or special preparations will be needed, especially if there is already a border in front of them, and where the soil is cultivated. Against the walls of houses or other buildings where the soil is often very poor, or where a gravelled or paved path is so close that there is little or no space for soil, then a considerable amount of preparation is necessary.

A space $1\frac{1}{2}$ to 2 feet (45–60 cm) wide and as much deep should be made at the base of the wall and filled with good top soil. If this is not available, dig in some well-decayed manure, compost, leafmould, rotted straw or peat moss, any of which will be of considerable help in improving the soil. On a heavy clay soil, it may be necessary to add a certain amount of coarse drainage material, in addition to some well-decayed compost, leafmould or coarse peat moss which will help to increase the aeration and improve the drainage of the soil.

The ideal soil is a good light alluvial loam to which is added a quantity of decayed leaves or peat moss. If the soil is free from lime chalk, this mixture will suit a wide variety of plants, including the peat loving kinds.

Once the soil has been prepared and improved in structure, it should be levelled and firmed by careful treading before planting. When the plant is taken from its container, the roots should be disturbed as litttle as possible. When, as sometimes happens, a plant has remained in the pot too long and the roots have become very congested and formed a ball, try to open out the roots a little before planting, although too much root disturbance can check the plant's growth. Plants which have become very pot bound or root restricted rarely grow away so freely as those which have a less cramped root system. Make sure, when buying plants, that you choose those with deep green leaves rather than those showing early signs of starvation, such as leaf yellowing. It is important to make sure that the soil is thoroughly moist at planting time. If necessary, soak the plant overnight in a bucket of water before planting.

Dig a hole wide enough and deep enough to take the roots, and plant with the soil level at the same place on the stem as it was in the container. Firm the soil around the roots.

After planting, the young plant should be secured to a strong stake or some other means of support, to prevent it being blown about by the wind. A good mulch of well-rotted straw, manure, or garden compost round the base of the plant will help to conserve moisture and to prevent drying out of the soil during periods of drought. In its first growing season it may also be necessary to give the young plant a good watering in dry periods. Often the ground at the base of the wall or fence becomes very dry through lack of adequate rain, and it is essential to keep the soil damp by watering.

As most plants are grown and sold in containers, planting can be done at any time of the year although autumn or early spring is to be preferred.

Below: the slightly tender *Cytisus battandieri* benefits from wall protection (see p.29).
Opposite above: *Carpentaria californica*, an evergreen flowering in June and July (see p. 23).
Opposite below left: *Cistus×purpureus*, one of the most decorative sun roses, is more likely to survive the winter against a wall (see p. 25).
Opposite below right: *Clematis* 'H. F. Young', one of the best blue flowered hybrids (see pp. 26–7).

Artificial support

There are many climbers and shrubs which do not possess natural means of supporting themselves and therefore some type of artificial support has to be given.

One of the commonest methods for brick walls is to use a specially stout type of non-rusting nails with strips of rubber backed pieces of canvas, strong cloth or other lasting material, such as plastic. Strong twine or tarred string can also be used in a similar way. The use of nails in the walls of dwelling houses or other buildings and walls is not altogether satisfactory and can be detrimental. Quite often during high winds, the extra weight on the branches caused by rain or heavy snowfalls will bring the supports, including the nails, from the wall. To avoid this the most satisfactory means of support is to fix stout galvanized wires horizontally to the wall, or in the case of twining climbers vertically, from 8 to 12 inches (20–30 cm) apart, held in position at regular intervals by hooked or eyelet-holed metal pins, known as vine eyes, driven into the wall. Strong galvanized hooks can also be used. Both types are available in shops, garden centres and nurseries.

Another method of support is a lattice work of narrow laths, painted or creosoted, and joined together in the form of frames, and wooden trellis work is equally effective. Both types can be easily fixed to the wall and held firm with the aid of wall plugs, screws or nails.

Strips of plastic-coated steel or wire netting fixed to the walls are also effective. This is very strong, resistant to rust and can be obtained in different mesh sizes and in various lengths. Much cheaper is the ordinary strong galvanized wire netting in various mesh sizes, but it is an advantage to give it a coat of bituminous paint before fixing to reduce rusting.

There are also other strong durable synthetic, polythene types of netting now available in various mesh sizes. They are easy to handle and cut to size, and are ideal supports for plants which do not make a heavy weight, such as *Lathyrus* (sweet pea) and *Ipomoea* (morning glory), which look very effective planted near the wall. Ordinary pea sticks can also be used.

A point to be remembered when dealing with vigorous climbers is that branches should be kept well clear of any gutters or drainpipes. The annual growth can easily be disentangled and removed, but with age the main stems of wisteria, for example, can be 6 inches (5 cm) or more in diameter, and can easily force a down-pipe or gutter away from the wall if allowed to grow behind it.

Using the above-mentioned methods of support some wall plants (including fruit trees, see pp. 59–62) are suitable for training into various forms, the most popular of which are fans and espaliers. The advantage of these forms is that the wall is well covered by the plant, which in turn is securely supported by wires, and this is less likely to be damaged in windy weather.

FAN TRAINING

This is a suitable method of training for a shrub such as *Ceanothus*, and all stone fruits, such as cherries, plums and peaches. During the first year after planting the main shoot is tied in vertically as it grows and the lateral shoots are fanned out to fill the available space as evenly as possible. In subsequent years the young shoots need to be tied in regularly during the spring and summer, and the previous season's growths should be pruned back after flowering. Annual regular pruning will maintain the shape of the mature plant.

ESPALIER

This method of training is suitable for ornamental shrubs, such as *Pyracantha*, and is often used for fruit trees. To train as an espalier, cut the young plant back to three good buds, with the two lower buds pointing in opposite directions. Tie the shoot from the top bud to a vertical support, and train the shoots from the other two buds along canes fixed at an angle of about 45° to the main stem. At the end of the growing season lower the two side branches to the horizontal wires and tie them in. Cut back the vertical leader to a bud about 18 inches (45 cm) above the lower arm, leaving two good buds to form the next horizontal arms. Cut back any surplus laterals on the main stem to three buds and prune back the lower horizontal arms by one-third, cutting to downward-facing buds. Repeat this process each year in the autumn until the shrub has filled the required space, and prune back the new terminal growths of the vertical and horizontal arms each summer, to keep the tree at its required size.

Above: the hardy *Abelia* × *grandiflora* flowers in late summer (see p.20).
Below: *Crinodendron hookeranum* with its attractive crimson lanterns
(see p.29).

Above: the Mexican orange blossom, *Choisya ternata*, (see p.25).
Below: *Coronilla glauca*, a useful member of the pea family, from southern Europe (see p.29).

Feeding

Many wall plants, once they are established and making good root growth, become strong, vigorous growers and will benefit by regular annual feeding. This is especially necessary if they are growing in poor or light gravelly soil where the essential plant foods quickly become leached out, or where the plants are growing in a narrow border along a wall or near buildings where there is little soil and the nutrients become exhausted.

Any of the organic manures, such as hoof and horn, fish or meal bone, can be used to supply the nutrients. These can be obtained in various grades, although the coarser grades are slower acting and are best applied to the plant during the late winter or very early spring months. If these are difficult to obtain a general fertilizer is recommended. These contain the three major plant nutrients, nitrogen, potassium and phosphate. A good dressing should be scattered around the root of the plant and surrounding soil (about 2–3 oz. per square yard (56–85 g per m²)) and lightly forked into the top few inches of soil. This should preferably be done during showery weather or when the soil is moist. If the soil is dry, as often is the case against walls or near buildings where it is difficult for rain to penetrate, then it may be necessary to give it a good watering after the fertilizer has been applied.

Mulching or top dressing the soil with some well-rotted manure, compost, or leafmould not only keeps the soil and plant roots relatively warm in winter and cool and moist in the summer, but it can also provide some nutrients. The mulch can either be left on the surface or it can be forked lightly into the top few inches of soil during the winter months, but care should be taken not to expose the roots above the soil surface when forking. For plants which have just been transplanted it is better to leave the mulch on the surface to help retain moisture and keep the roots cool during the summer rather than fork it in.

With camellias and other plants which prefer plenty of leafmould and peat in the soil, there is nothing better than a good annual top dressing of decayed leaves which provide a natural feed for this particular class of plant.

Pruning

Plants which are grown on a wall usually have to be kept within certain limits. To do this the plants need a periodical, usually annual, pruning or training, which is dependent on two factors, the amount of space available and time of flowering. With regard to space this depends both on the area of wall available and on the distance the shrub can be allowed to grow out from the wall. Sometimes plants growing on walls are pruned too much and are kept too close against the wall; how much better to see a well-grown shrub with its branches standing out 1 or 2 feet (30–60 cm) from the wall. It is better to choose a plant which is amenable to training, rather than having to keep continually pruning.

The time to prune depends on the time of year that the plant flowers and the type of growth. Climbers and shrubs can be divided roughly into two groups; those that flower on the current season's shoots, generally from midsummer onwards to the autumn, and those that flower from March to June on shoots made the previous summer.

In the first group pruning consists of cutting back the shoots that have flowered, if possible to a dormant bud near the base. This should be done in late winter or early spring (February–March) so as to give the plant the longest possible period for growing before flowering later in the year; examples of this group are *Clematis* × *jackmanii* types, some types of *Buddleja*, and *Caryopteris*.

The second group includes those that flower on the growth made in the previous summer; pruning should be done immediately after flowering, cutting back the strong growths which have just flowered to encourage new shoots. These will produce buds to flower in the following season. Sufficient young shoots should also be left, on which flower buds will be formed for the following year. Examples of this group are *Ceanothus*, *Buddleja davidii*, *Forsythia*, *Prunus triloba* and *Clematis montana*.

This hard annual pruning is not necessary for all plants. There are quite a number of plants which are not vigorous growers and make comparatively little growth every year, and they require little or no pruning, certainly no annual pruning, only tying in the new growth as it develops. Young plants that are in the early stages of being trained up a wall need only very light pruning each year to encourage branching and stimulate more growth on which the framework of the plant is built up. It is only when it has reached its maximum height and allotted space that it may be necessary to prune harder.

For plants which are grown primarily for their foliage or autumn colour, such as vines or variegated shrubs, the time of pruning is less important. The most favourable times are winter for deciduous plants and early spring for evergreens, with possibly a second pruning in August to thin out redundant or overcrowded shoots.

While pruning is being done it is wise to cut out any dead or weak shoots and to check and renew where necessary old or weak ties which support the main framework. It is also important to make a regular inspection of all plants during the growing season and tie in new shoots. Often, uncontrolled growths become intertwined with one another, making it difficult to sort them out at the end of the growing season.

Fuller details of pruning requirements are given in *Pruning Ornamental Shrubs*, also published in the Wisley Handbook Series.

Prunus triloba should be cut back immediately after flowering (see p.46).

Winter protection

One of the reasons for growing a plant against a wall is to give some extra protection to plants that would be killed or damaged by a winter in the open. Some of these plants may need additional cover in their first few winters, until they become established.

It is difficult to cover completely half-hardy or tender shrubs which have grown to more than five feet (1.5 m) high, unless it is something really very special. The main aim with established plants is to protect the lower parts of the stem and branches up to about 3 feet (90 cm) from the ground, from which new growth can develop in spring if the unprotected parts of the plant are injured or killed by frost.

The time to put on the covering depends on the weather. Severe weather before December or even January is unusual, and the longer that covering is delayed the more acclimatized to low temperatures the plants will become. But, to be on the safe side, the plants should be covered by the end of November. Remove the protection in early March, when the weather has usually started to warm up.

Probably the best and most convenient material to use is dried bracken that has been cut in late autumn. If this is not obtainable short straw is quite effective. Tuck the material lightly in around the lower branches, allowing air to circulate freely through the material so that it remains relatively dry at all times; this is an important factor during frost. A few stakes and some twine will help to keep the material in position. The use of dead stems such as Michaelmas daisies, *Solidago* and similar material cut from the herbaceous border, can also be effectively used in the same way.

Another method quite often adopted and one which can be used for several successive winters, is to place a thick layer of bracken, straw or other similar material between lengths of small mesh galvanized wire netting or polythene film, which is firmly tied together to keep the material in position. The netting can then be cut into various lengths as required and held in position by a few stakes. Pieces of sacking or coconut matting can be cut into the required lengths and used in a similar way.

With plants of a semi-prostrate habit the material can be lightly worked in and around the stems and if necessary held in position with a few short upright stakes.

Perennial climbing and wall plants

Abelia floribunda is the most tender and the most beautiful of the abelias, having rosy red, pendulous, funnel-shaped flowers borne on long arching stems during June and July. For a south or west wall this shrub with its shining leaves is most attractive.

Abelia × grandiflora, which is hardier, has white and pink blossoms, and flowers from July until the autumn; it has a very graceful habit and is most useful flowering so late in the season. Both species mentioned are reasonably slow growing but eventually reach a height of 5 to 6 feet (1.5–1.8 m) and more in very sheltered localities. It is hardy except in severe winters (see p.14).

Abeliophyllum distichum originates from Korea, and is related to *Forsythia* (see p. 31). It is a comparatively slow growing, hardy but dainty deciduous twiggy shrub, which grows to about 4 feet (1.2 m) high. The small flowers are fragrant, white tinged pink and freely produced on short racemes. Unfortunately it starts to flower at the end of January and is liable to be damaged by frost; on a south wall there is less danger of this.

Abutilon megapotamicum, although a native of Brazil, makes a very graceful evergreen shrub for growing in a sheltered position, where it will come through an average winter unharmed. It is an advantage to give some protection around the base of the plant, using either dried bracken fronds, straw, or similar material, as a precaution. The bright red and yellow pendulous flowers are produced on long slender arching growths from the leaf axils, throughout the summer. There is also a variegated form which has leaves blotched with bright yellow (see p.6).

Abutilon vitifolium is an altogether larger, more upright shrub, which requires a sheltered, sunny position. The saucer-shaped flowers, which are pale to deep mauve and continue in bloom from May to July, are well set off by the vine-shaped greyish leaves. In recent years it has been crossed with *A. ochsenii*, a weaker growing species from Chile but with beautifully shaped violet flowers. The hybrid, × *suntense* is as vigorous as *A. vitifolium* and hardier. The flowers have the better shape and deeper violet of *A. ochensii*. All three plants benefit from wall protection in colder gardens but are unsuitable for training on a wall (see p.2).

Actinidia chinensis, a deciduous climber introduced from

China in 1900, is very vigorous and will if required grow up a tree. It is worth growing for its large, handsome heart-shaped leaves. Its creamy buff-yellow flowers are sometimes followed in Britain by brown, edible fruits the size of an egg, sold as Kiwi fruit. Both sexes are necessary to obtain fruits (see p.6).

Actinidia kolomikta is a deciduous species from China, Japan and Manchuria, which is not as vigorous as some other species. It is well worth growing for the attraction of its leaves which when fully developed have a large area of pink and white variegation at the tips.

Akebia is an Asiatic genus of two species of vigorous, deciduous climbers with racemes of small, dark purple or purple-brown flowers, which in some years are followed by violet, sausage-shaped fruits. In A. *lobata* the leaves are composed of three leaflets while those of A. *quinata* are made up of five leaflets. In both species the foliage is elegant, but they require space.

Ampelopsis brevipedunculata, a luxuriant climber from eastern Asia, has deeply lobed and bristly leaves like those of the hop. It is attractive in autumn with its branches of small bright blue grapes. Its clone 'Elegans' (also known as A. *heterophylla* var. *variegata*) is far less strong growing and has handsome leaves which are mottled white and pink, with pinkish young shoots. This also needs a more sheltered position and is better suited to the milder counties. It is sometimes sold as a houseplant.

Aristolochia macrophylla (also known as A. *sipho*) is a plant grown chiefly for its foliage effect. It is commonly called Dutchman's pipe on account of the flowers being shaped like a dutch pipe. They are about 1 to 2 inches (2–5 cm) long, tubular, inflated and yellowish green in colour; the flat expanding lobes at the end of the flowers are brownish purple. It is a very vigorous climber, and is useful for quick coverage. The large, kidney-shaped leaves are deciduous.

Berberidopsis corallina, sometimes known as the coral plant, is beautiful when well grown. As a native of Chile it is not really hardy and only suited for the milder parts of the country. It needs a very sheltered and preferably a cool shady position, in a rich, lime-free soil. It is an evergreen shrub with heart shaped, dark green leaves and large pendent globular coral red flowers produced in the axils of the uppermost leaves in beautiful drooping racemes. It is not self supporting and it is necessary therefore to tie the leading shoots to some sort of support.

Buddleja colvilei, which originates from the Himalayas, will reach almost tree-like dimensions in cultivation. It has large lance-shaped leaves and drooping panicles of substantial rose to rosy crimson bell-shaped flowers, which are borne on mature growths. It should never be pruned annually or cut back in early spring as is the case with the well-known *B. davidii (variabilis)*. Care is needed, and space, if it is to be trained on a wall. It is admirable when planted in the angle of two walls where it should be allowed to develop without restraint. It is tender when young and requires some winter protection until well established (see p.7).

The genus **Camellia** contains a wide variety of excellent flowering evergreen shrubs, suited not only for woodland planting but also useful for growing on walls. There is space here to deal only with a number of the less hardy species and some of the more recent hybrids which, because they flower when frosts are prevalent, derive benefit from the shelter of walls. *Camellia cuspidata* has a distinctive habit, with slender growths, small white flowers and copper-tinted young growths. It has been largely superseded by its hybrid 'Cornish Snow', which has rather larger flowers produced in greater profusion from March onwards, while retaining much of the quiet charm of its parent.

There are innumerable cultivars of the Japanese *C. sasanqua* grown in its native land and such warm climates as that of California. In this country one cultivar alone, 'Nurumi-gata', with flowers resembling those of the Christmas rose, blooms with sufficient regularity to warrant its use on valuable wall space. It is of value as it produces its attractive flowers from October onwards.

Two related Chinese species *C. reticulata* and *C. saluenensis* show considerable variation in size of leaf and in shape and tone of their pink flowers. Except in very mild areas wall protection is essential if they are to succeed and, like the species and hybrids already mentioned, they are well worth the shelter of a west or north-west wall, particularly where an unusual plant is desired. A hybrid between these two species, 'Francie L' is well suited to training on walls and bears beautiful large, deep rose-coloured flowers.

Camellia saluenensis crossed with *C. japonica*, has produced a race of hybrids known collectively as *C. × williamsii*, with almost unparalleled freedom of flower, surprising hardiness and other good qualities. They start to flower when young plants, and most of them have the advantage of shedding their flowers as soon as they fade or become damaged. In the south they do not need the protection of a wall, but as they flower when frost is prevalent the shelter of a wall may ensure a successful display of flowers and their pinks and rosy reds will lighten many a dull wall. The following are some of the best cultivars:

'Donation' upright habit.
'E. G. Waterhouse', upright habit, formal double, pink.

'George Blandford', low, spreading, early, but long in flower, semi-double, rosy red.

'J. C. Williams', horizontal branching, single flat, blush pink.

'Lady Gowrie', compact, vigorous, large semi-double pink.

'November Pink', open habit, earliest to flower, but continuously in flower, single, funnel-shaped, pink.

'Parkside', open, spreading, single, clear pink.

'St Ewe', erect, single, funnel-shaped, rosy red.

Camellia × *williamsii* 'Donation' is considered to be one of the most outstanding camellias. However, equally outstanding is 'Leonard Messel', in which the semi-double pink flowers have a hint of coral. Although a hybrid of the tender *C. reticulata* with *C.* × *williamsii* 'Mary Christian', it is apparently as hardy as 'Donation'.

All camellias like a good moisture-retentive soil, well drained, but free from lime, and preferably one to which peat or leafmould has been added; they will not succeed on a chalk soil. Little pruning is required apart from an occasional thinning of overcrowded growth, dead wood and regular tying in of new growth. (See also the Wisley Handbook *Camellias*.)

Campsis is yet another genus of vigorous, deciduous climbers, which can be spectacular when covered with orange or orange-red, trumpet-shaped flowers. Unfortunately in Britain we do not enjoy sufficient regular hot summers to produce flowers in profusion and they are perhaps better when seen in southern Europe. *Campsis radicans* supports itself by aerial roots and may attain a height of 30–40 feet (9–12 cm). There is a hybrid 'Madame Galen' which is hardier than its parents. (*C. grandiflora* and *C. radicans*) and bears salmon-red flowers. Campsis should be planted against a south or west-facing wall.

Carpenteria californica is an evergreen shrub with a neat habit of growth reaching a height of 5 to 6 feet (1.5–1.8 m). It requires a sunny position (preferably facing south) and good drainage. The large white flowers contrasting with the golden anthers, are borne in June and July in terminal clusters of from three to six. These are 2 to 3 inches (5–7 cm) wide with five rounded petals (see p. 11).

The genus **Ceanothus** contains mostly evergreen shrubs with flowers of varying shades of blue and purple. They are native to the warm regions of California, Colorado and New Mexico where they get plenty of sunshine and hot dry conditions. Most of them prefer a light, well-drained sandy soil on a sunny south wall, but also succeed on walls facing west or east.

One of the most popular is *C.* × *veitchianus*, a spreading bush up to 10 feet (3 m) high, with small roundish glossy green leaves and dense heads of bright blue flowers produced during May and

June. *Ceanothus rigidus* has small glossy, holly-shaped leaves and deep purplish blue flowers borne in great profusion during April and May.

Another easy species is *C. dentatus* which has small oval leaves, bright green above but covered with a close grey felt on the underside. The brilliant blue flowers are produced in clusters in May. Another distinct plant, grown under the name of *Ceanothus impressus*, is considered by some to be a variety of *C. dentatus*. It is very close growing, with very small leaves and rich blue flowers. It quickly attains a height of 10 to 12 feet (3–3.6 m).

A very fine, early flowering species worthy of its place is *C. thyrsiflorus* which is a stronger growing type with larger, more rounded, glossy green leaves about $1\frac{1}{2}$ to 2 inches long and 1 inch wide (5 × 2.5 cm). The pale blue flowers are borne in clusters on long stalks from the leaf axils of the previous season's growth.

Equally attractive and vigorous but inclined to be less hardy is *C. griseus*. Its large oval shaped leaves are similar in size but dull grey green on the under surface; the flowers are a pale lilac shade making it a very attractive plant when in flower in May.

All those *Ceanothus* which flower in early spring do so on the growth which has been made the previous season. It is therefore very important to carry out any pruning which may be necessary immediately after flowering, shortening back the growths which have flowered to within a few inches of their base.

There are a few other species which flower in summer on growth made during the current season; for this group, which includes the popular 'Gloire de Versailles', pruning has to be done in early spring (March-April). Strong shoots are shortened back to two or three buds from the base.

Celastrus orbiculatus, a twining climber, is related to the spindle berries and like them has small, highly decorative yellow and red fruits. It is very robust and apart from the necessity to plant both male and female plants, requires a lot of space. The leaves turn yellow before falling.

The genus **Chaenomeles** is a useful group of deciduous shrubs, which although perfectly hardy, look very attractive when grown as wall plants. Given a warm sunny position they will often come into flower early in the spring, and will also succeed in conditions of partial shade, such as on north-east or west walls. Regular pruning of wall plants will improve their flowering. Cut back the side shoots to two or three buds aftrer flowering is over.

Chaenomeles speciosa (the well-known early flowering "japonica") is very vigorous; there are different kinds producing flowers in all shades of red, pink or white from March or early

May. Some clones such as 'Simonii' are dwarfer with more pendulous branches and flat, blood red or scarlet flowers. They and *C. japonica* have a spreading habit and do not normally grow more than 3 feet (90 cm), thus being ideal for planting against low walls or under windows where wall space is restricted.

A race of hybrids, named *C. × superba*, has been raised by crossing *C. japonica* with *C. speciosa* and can be trained up to 6 feet (1.8 m) or more on walls. Often clones of the species and hybrids are grouped together in catalogues. They include 'Crimson and Gold', red with golden stamens; 'Moerloosii', pink and white; 'Knap Hill Scarlet', orange-red; 'Nivalis', pure white; 'Phylis Moore', almond-pink; 'Rowallane', blood-red (see p.33).

Chimonanthus praecox, the well-known winter sweet, is a very old and delightful shrub introduced from China as far back as 1766, since when it has been a great favourite because of its sweetly scented flowers. Although perfectly hardy it benefits from the warmth of a sunny wall. It flowers from December and intermittently until March depending on the weather. The flowers are borne on the previous summer's growth, with the outer petals greenish yellow, the inner ones purplish, and each about one inch across. They have no particular beauty but are valued for their fragrance and early flowering. The clone 'Luteus' has larger flowers. Regular pruning is not needed but long shoots may be pruned no later than March.

Choisya ternata, Mexican orange blossom, is another useful shrub for planting where it can receive plenty of sun and shelter from cold east winds which may damage the growth in some winters. It is an evergreen of rounded bushy habit 6 to 9 feet (1.8–2.7 m) high, requiring ample space to develop. The leaves are glossy green, 3 to 6 inches (7–15 cm) long, composed of two to three leaflets. The white fragrant flowers are borne in clusters of three to five during April and May on the previous year's growth, and occasionally again during the late summer (see p.15).

Another very useful and decorative group of sun-loving, evergreen plants is **Cistus**; all appreciate a hot sheltered position and thrive in light well-drained soil. Most are native to the Mediterranean, and as one would expect may suffer badly during a very severe winter. Most flower from May to July.

One of the most striking is *C. × purpureus* which has leathery leaves and large bright rose-purple flowers with a conspicuous chocolate basal blotch. It makes a rounded bush up to 5 to 6 feet (1.5–1.8 m) high (see p.11).

Cistus ladanifer is a beautiful, erect species up to 6 feet (1.8 m) high, with sticky, lance-shaped leaves. The flowers are white, with a crimson zoning at the base.

Cistus × *pulverulentus*, sometimes called 'Sunset', makes a compact shrub of 2 to 3 feet (60–90 cm) high, with grey-green hairy leaves, and rosy pink flowers about 2 inches (5 cm) wide.

Cistus × *skanbergii* forms a dense twiggy shrub up to 4 feet (1.2 m) high, with grey-green leaves and small shell pink flowers in terminal clusters.

These are but a few of a large group. Their disadvantage is that they are short-lived, although new plants can easily be raised from cuttings. These are best taken in August after flowering using short soft wooded nodal cuttings 2 to 3 inches (5–7 cm) in length and rooted in sandy soil (1 part soil to 3 parts of silver sand), or some other rooting medium, in a cold or if possible a slightly heated frame.

There is no cultivated genus of climbers to equal **Clematis**, a very useful and extensive group of wall plants which, when in flower, provide some of the most beautiful effects one could wish for in a garden. The various types provide blooms for many months during the summer starting from June until the end of September, but although they are perfectly hardy, the young growth may occasionally be damaged by late spring frosts. They provide a great variety of colour particularly among the hybrids of the large flowered types ranging from white, blue, purple, and mauve to red and pink. They constitute the most important section of the genus.

These hybrids are not difficult to grow, succeeding in a retentive but well-drained, loamy, calcareous soil, although all of them – including many of the species – will thrive quite well in soil which does not contain lime. The best time to plant is during the autumn, in October or November; if this is not possible, plant in early spring before new growth starts. Once planted they should be left undisturbed at the roots and when established will continue and flower regularly every year. They are all sun lovers, but the lower part of the main stem should preferably be shaded; this can be done by planting near the base of the plant a dwarf shrub which will cast some light shade and allow the clematis to grow up through it. With the exception of more tender species like *C. armandii* they generally do well in every aspect except dense shade.

The selection of these hybrids is a matter of personal choice. However, among the best are 'Barbara Dibley', pansy violet with petunia bars; 'Barbara Jackman', soft petunia with plum colour bars; 'Beauty of Worcester', deep violet blue; 'Captain Thuilleaux' cream with deep pink bars; 'Comtesse de Bouchaud', soft mauve pink; 'Duchess of Edinburgh', double white; 'Elsa Spath', deep lavender; 'Hagley Hybrid', deep shell pink; 'H. F. Young,

Wedgwood blue; 'Huldine', translucent white with pink bands on the reverse; 'Jackmanii', deep violet; 'Lasurstern', rich blue; 'Marie Boisselot', pure white; 'Mrs Cholmondely', lavender blue; 'Nellie Moser', mauve pink with carmine bands; 'The President', deep violet; 'Perle d'Azur', pale blue; 'Ville de Lyon', deep carmine-red. Those cultivars with contrasting bars or bands are best grown with a north-west aspect if the colours are not to fade in the sun (see p. 11).

Among the large number of species in cultivation there are some which I consider just as attractive and as easy to grow. Foremost is *Clematis montana*, probably one of the most beautiful Asiatic deciduous species ever to have been introduced. It is very vigorous, growing 15 to 20 feet (4.5–6 m) high and even more if allowed to do so. Its white flowers are borne in great profusion during May and June in axillary clusters on long growths made the previous year. There are also several very good forms, such as *rubens*, with the same vigorous growth and rosy pink flowers; 'Elizabeth', large pearly pink flowers, sweetly scented; 'Tetrarose', extra large pink flowers which retain their colour to maturity, followed by purplish green foliage; and the variety *wilsonii* which has very large white flowers produced much later in the season. Any pruning to be done to these early flowering types should not be done until after flowering, cutting back the shoots that have flowered almost to their base.

Another species worth growing is *C. chrysocoma*, with white flowers tinged pink opening in May and June, and quite often again in late summer on the new growth. The leaves, flower stalks and very young shoots are covered with a fine yellowish silky down which gives the plant an attractive appearance. One of its chief merits for a small garden is that it is less rampant than *Clematis montana*.

Clematis armandii is a beautiful Chinese species, a strong grower well worth planting for its handsome evergreen, dark green leathery trifoliate leaves and cluster of creamy white sweetly scented flowers opening in early spring. It is liable to injury in severe winters and therefore demands a sheltered sunny position on a wall. It requires very little pruning, but care should be taken when tying in new growth which is often brittle and breaks readily. There are two very good cultivars, 'Snowdrift' a good white, and 'Apple Blossom' which has broad petals delicately shaded pink.

Where space is limited *Clematis macropetala* is a very charming species to grow. It has a much more slender type of growth ultimately reaching a height of 6 to 10 feet (1.8–3 m). The flowers are solitary on growth made in the previous year, usually powder

27

blue in colour, although seedlings vary considerably. There is a cultivar called 'Markham's Pink' which has very nice pink flowers and is well worth growing. Although this species is quite hardy it does look most attractive when trained on a wall, fence or pergola while in some gardens it seems to thrive better if given a semi-shady position, supporting itself on some other shrub.

Another very delightful deciduous Chinese species is *C. tangutica*. It is quite hardy, but well suited for training up a wall, or planted near some other light shrub or climber where its slender growth can ramble at will. It produces an abundance of solitary yellow flowers from July onwards, followed by attractive round feathery seed heads. Another yellow flowered species is *Clematis tibetana* subsp. *vernayi* (LS&E No. 13342) known as 'Orange Peel' with four thick, waxy yellow sepals.

The method of pruning depends (a) on the position and space they are intended to occupy and (b) on their time and mode of flowering. The early flowering types such as *C. montana* and its varieties, *C. armandii* and *C. macropetala*, do not need regular pruning, but, if necessary, are pruned as soon as possible after flowering. The amount of pruning is related to the space the plant is to occupy. Once the allotted space has been filled then it may be necessary to cut hard back to old woody stems particularly if the plant becomes top heavy and growth a tangled mass. All new growth made after pruning should be carefully tied into position where required.

The later flowering types like *C. × jackmanii* and *C. lanuginosa* cultivars, which flower on the current year's growth, are pruned during February, cutting back the old flowering stems to growth buds which will by this time be large enough to show which parts of the stems are alive or dead. Occasionally it is advisable to cut a small proportion of the stems well back so that the new shoots will be stimulated to grow from the lower parts of the plant which so often remain bare. Great care should be taken when tying in new shoots, which, being soft and brittle, are easily broken. (See also the Wisley Handbook *Clematis*.)

Clianthus puniceus is a slightly tender shrub from New Zealand, and therefore prefers a south or west-facing wall. If provided with warmth and a well-drained soil it will produce bright red flowers, looking somewhat like a lobster's claw, during June and July. Winter protection, using bracken, straw or polythene is advisable in northern areas of Britain. It grows to about 8 feet (2.4 m) and can be propagated by seed sown in spring, or by cuttings taken during the summer.

Another very useful low growing shrub of 2 to 3 feet (60–90 cm) is **Convolvulus cneorum**, a south European species, with lovely silver foliage which makes a good foil to the white and blush-pink, funnel-shaped flowers in summer. It loves a hot dry sunny position in well drained soil. I have seen it growing and flowering with great freedom on chalky soil.

Coronilla glauca belongs to the pea family and is from south Europe. It is an attractive plant for a warm sunny sheltered position, making a neat bush up to 5 feet (1.5 m) high with clusters of rich yellow pea-shaped flowers which contrast with the glaucous green pinnate leaves. It is a plant with a long flowering period from April until June and quite often a second flush in autumn (see p.15).

Cotoneaster horizontalis always makes a charming shrub in whatever position it is placed. Normally if grown in the open it spreads horizontally but it is attractive when allowed to grow upwards and trained against a wall to show off its characteristic 'herringbone' habit of branching. Each autumn it can be relied upon to give masses of bright red berries with rich autumn foliage. It is a good plant for a north or east facing wall.

With the right growing conditions, particularly in the milder parts, and sufficient space, every endeavour should be made to grow at least one specimen of **Crinodendron**. The most attractive species is the evergreen *Crinodendron hookerianum*, it grows into a large shrub that produces urn-shaped flowers during early summer which hang from the branches like crimson lanterns in contrast to the deep green lance-shaped leaves. It requires a cool moist lime-free soil of loam and peat, and needs a very sheltered warm wall shaded from the hot midday sun (see p.14).

The Moroccan **Cytisus battandieri** is a vigorous, loose-growing shrub, or small tree, up to 15 feet (4.5 m) high, which although it is hardy in the southern counties, is an excellent plant for training on sunny walls. The leaves are laburnum-like and covered with a silky, silvery sheen. The yellow flowers are scented of pineapple and are carried in erect cone-shaped clusters on the current year's growth in June or July. It does not need hard pruning, and only unnecessary or dead wood should be removed. It is usually raised from seed, which is often set freely, and seedlings may take a considerable number of years before flowering. They also show some variation, some being more prolific in flowering than others (see p.10).

Dendromecon rigida is a beautiful, evergreen, rather tender shrub which needs a warm, sunny wall. It requires a light, well-drained soil, and, if happy, can reach a height of up to 15 feet (4.6 m). The bright yellow, poppy-like flowers are borne from spring to autumn.

A plant from South America is **Desfontainea spinosa**, a

very large beautiful evergreen shrub with small holly-like leaves. The large conspicuous red and orange tubular flowers are produced singly from the leaf axils from July to September. It will come through most winters unharmed in the milder counties of the south and west, and many fine specimens are to be seen about the country growing against a wall. It appears to thrive on a wall sheltered from hot sun and in cool lime-free soil (see p.64).

Eccremocarpus scaber is a charming semi-woody climber growing 5 to 6 feet (1.5–1.8 m) high in favourable conditions. The plant climbs by the tendrils produced by the pinnate leaves. From June onwards long racemes of up to a dozen bright orange, yellow or red tubular flowers about one inch (2.5 cm) long are produced until late in the summer (see p.36).

It was introduced into this country late in 1824, and not being completely hardy is well suited for growing on a south or west wall. In some colder areas, young seedlings may have to be raised each year. This is easily done by sowing early in the spring in a little heat, hardening off and then planting out in a permanent position to flower the same season.

Another distinct member of the pea family is **Erythrina crista-galli**, perhaps better known as the coral tree; it likes a warm sunny position against a wall. Established plants have a thick woody rootstock from which are produced strong annual shoots 6 to 8 feet (1.8–2.4 m) long; these bear oval leathery leaflets more or less glaucous green, terminating in a large inflorescence of conspicuous deep scarlet flowers in autumn. To encourage strong healthy flowering shoots the following season, these long annual growths should be cut hard back to within a few inches of the base of the rootstock each spring before new growth begins. Being a native of Brazil this plant is only half-hardy in most parts of the country, and therefore the rootstock must be covered with some form of protection against severe frost (see p.33).

Of the many attractive hybrids of the South American genus **Escallonia**, the finest and most suitable as a wall shrub is E. × iveyi. It has dark green, oval leaves, which are typically glossy, and large, pyramidal panicles of white flowers in late summer and autumn. It can make a large rounded shrub after many years, but there is a fine specimen some 6 to 7 feet (1.8–2.1 m) high growing on a south wall at Kew, which has survived many winters.

Euonymus fortunei var. **radicans** is a creeping shrub which will grow up to 15 feet (4.5 m) on a house wall. The plant is as useful as ivy in covering large areas of wall, and will grow in the same sort of conditions, growing well in sunny or shaded positions. It is grown as a foliage plant, and in its climbing state does not produce flowers.

There is also a variegated cultivar 'Variegatus', which has a white band along both sides of the leaves. It is a colourful plant in spring when the new leaves are produced. There is another variegated cultivar called 'Silver Queen'.

Fabiana imbricata is a very charming evergreen with heath-like foliage belonging to the potato family. It is a Chilean shrub for a warm sunny position, having slender racemes of long, narrow, white, tubular-shaped flowers each $\frac{1}{2}$ to $\frac{3}{4}$ inch (12–19 mm) long produced in June.

I well remember a fine specimen of it, 6 to 8 feet (1.8–2.4 m) high, growing and flowering freely each year, on a sheltered west wall at the Cambridge Botanic Garden. There it survived several hard winters unharmed, in a light gravelly soil containing a high percentage of lime. Equally attractive and of similar appearance is the variety *violacea* with flowers of a pale shade of mauve, which is hardier in some localities.

Feijoa sellowiana is an evergreen shrub, which, being slightly tender, prefers a south or south-west facing wall. It will grow up to 15 feet (4.6 m) and has dark, grey-green leaves, which, together with the flower stalks, are covered with a white felt. The flowers are red and white, with conspicuous crimson stamens, and these are borne in July. *Feijoa* can be propagated by means of cuttings taken in July or August, and raised in a heated greenhouse.

All species and hybrids of **Forsythia** in cultivation are perfectly hardy but one species, *F. suspensa*, is particularly effective when it flowers in early spring, if trained on a north or east facing wall. It will grow up to 15 feet (4.5 m) high and requires ample space if it is to be well trained. Its variety *sieboldii* has golden yellow flowers and those of var. *atrocaulis* are pale lemon yellow, which are most attractive hanging from the black stems.

The training and pruning of a young forsythia to cover a given area of wall space requires several years of patience, although this can also be said of other plants as well. In its early stages it involves careful pruning to selected growth buds to encourage strong healthy stems or leaders which will form the framework to tie in these strong growths to the wall during their growing period in whichever direction they are required, in the same way as one would train a young fruit tree up a wall (see *espalier*, p. 13).

Immediately after flowering prune the leading shoots back to about half their length to two or three selected buds which will produce further strong shoots which are tied in during the current year. This same process of pruning and tying in subsequent growth is repeated until the whole allotted space is filled. In the meanwhile lateral growths will have been bearing flowers, and these should be pruned back immediately after flowering to a bud within 2 or 3 inches (5–7 cm) of the base of that year's growth. This method of pruning is repeated each year after flowering to encourage new flowering growth, and it also helps to keep the plant reasonably confined to the wall and prevents a lot of untidy straggly growth. This training and method of pruning can also be applied to *Prunus triloba* (see p. 46), *Chaenomeles* (see p. 24) and similar spring flowering plants.

The two species of **Fremontodendron** (until recently called *Fremontia*), *F. californicum* and *F. mexicanum*, are distinctly tender but well worth growing where there is space on a warm, sunny wall, for they often reach the roof in the south west. They are semi-deciduous with three-lobed leaves, felted on the under surface as are the stems with rust-coloured hairs, and slightly greyed above. The flowers appear in the summer, their great beauty being really bright yellow, rounded calyces, which in *F. mexicanum* are narrow and rather star-like.

There is now a hybrid of American origin between these two species called 'California Glory'; it is a strong, free flowering plant worth growing and is widely available through the trade; it is also hardier.

Garrya elliptica is an evergreen bushy shrub vigorous in growth once established, 6 to 10 feet (1.8–3 m) high when grown on a wall, and higher in the milder parts of the country. Its leaves are more or less round, dark shiny green above and grey-woolly beneath, from the axils of which are produced long slender hanging male catkins 3 to 5 inches (7.6–12 cm) in length, on which the greenish silvery clusters of flowers are formed. These catkins look most attractive from November to February at a time of the year when there is little of interest in the garden. The catkins of the female flowers, which are on separate plants, are much shorter and less attractive.

I have also seen good healthy specimens growing on walls with a northern and east facing aspect which is rather surprising considering the species is a native of California and Oregon.

Cistus and *Halimium* are closely related and have produced the bigeneric hybrid × **Halimiocistus wintonensis**. It is a very useful plant for the front of a border at the foot of a sunny wall as it only grows about 2 feet (60 cm) high and its grey leaves and large white flowers with a maroon and yellow basal blotch are attractive.

Halimium lasianthum is a similar plant, rather taller and with small silvery leaves, among which the yellow flowers, each with a chocolate blotch at the base, are very pretty. In the variety *concolor* the flowers are without blotches and about 2 inches (5 cm) across as are those of the species and hybrid (see p.36).

There are innumerable species and hybrids of the genus **Hebe**.

Above: *Erythrina crista-galli*, the coral tree, from Brazil (see p. 30).
Below left: *Chaenomeles × superba* 'Knap Hill Scarlet', with abundant, large, brilliant red flowers, is one of several hybrids in this group (see p. 25).
Below right: *Fremontodendron californicum* is an unusual summer flowering shrub but not reliably hardy (see opposite).

All are shrubby and evergreen, some are almost prostrate and others are big, bold shrubs with large leaves.

Among these large leaved hebes there is a group with colourful flowers generally known as *speciosa* hybrids, which are well worth growing if space is available under the shelter of a wall. There they will flower all summer long and form round bushes about 5 to 6 feet (1.5–1.8 m) high. Among the best of them are 'Alicia Amherst', deep purple; 'Gloriosa', bright pink; 'Purple Queen', bronze-tinted foliage, rosy purple; and 'Simon Delaux', rich crimson. All are somewhat tender.

Of the species of moderate height *H. hulkeana* is the most attractive with lustrous, green leaves and loose spikes up to one foot (30 cm) long, each bearing many small lavender flowers in May and June. It will grow to 3 or 4 feet (90–120 cm) high.

Hedera helix, the common ivy, is very well known. It is a very popular and adaptable plant, that will grow in almost any conditions from dense shade to full sunlight and in any type of soil. It also makes good ground cover providing it is kept within bounds. There is a considerable number of varieties ranging from those with white or yellow variagations, and there are also wide variations in the size and shape of the leaves, some being most attractive.

Two other beautiful ivies which should be mentioned are, first, the variegated form of *Hedera canariensis*, the Canary Island ivy, called 'Variegata' or 'Gloire de Marengo'. It is a strong grower with large rounded leaves, green in the centre, but merging into silvery grey irregular markings with a whitish border around the edge. The leaves may be injured in exposed cold windswept localities. The other is the variegated form of *Hedera colchica*, the Persian ivy ('Dentata Variegata'), having thick heart-shaped leaves up to 6 inches (15 cm) broad and as much long, often green shades in the middle with very conspicuous pale yellow to cream irregular variegations towards the outside of the leaves. This is the most handsome of all the large leaved ivies and is quite hardy.

Hoheria lyallii is a large, deciduous, branching shrub, with heart-shaped leaves and white flowers produced in July. *Hoheria glabrata* is similar in growth and flower but is considered to be hardier, while *H. sexstylosa* is a handsome evergreen which is sometimes defoliated in cold winters, but quickly recovers.

The genus **Holboellia** contains five species of evergreen climbers, of which only one, *H. coriacea*, is hardy in Britain. This species is vigorous, growing up to 20 feet (6 m) or more, and has twining stems which bear dark green glossy trifoliate leaves. The male flowers, which usually appear in April, are purplish in colour, while the female flowers are greenish white and appear a little later. Both types of flower are borne on the same plant.

The climbing hydrangea, **Hydrangea petiolaris**, will cover a large area, and flower profusely even on a north wall. It is very hardy and will cling closely to walls by means of the aerial roots produced on its stem. It is deciduous with rich green, egg-shaped pointed leaves which have sharply toothed edges and turn a pleasing shade of pale yellow in the autumn. The flattish heads of greenish white flowers are edged with conspicuous, white, sterile florets. It is an accommodating plant and will grow successfully in every aspect.

Honeysuckle (see *Lonicera*, p. 38).

An unusual shrub is **Itea ilicifolia**, a native of central China, an evergreen with shiny holly-like leaves. The small greenish white flowers are borne on extremely elegant slender drooping racemes 6 to 9 inches (15–20 cm) long during August. A young plant over five feet (1.5 m) high and as much across is growing at Kew in a narrow border facing south, sheltered at the back by a wall. It certainly makes an excellent wall plant, but perhaps not so colourful as many other plants (see p.37).

Ivy (see *Hedera*, opposite).

Probably the best known of the jasmines is **Jasminum officinale**, the common, white, sweetly scented jasmine, which has been cultivated in gardens for so long that the date of its introduction is forgotten. It is a native of Iran and countries eastwards as far as Kashmir and China. It is hardy in the south of England and it lends itself admirably to training up walls and pillars, looking most effective in flower when its long shoots bearing sprays of pure white blossoms are growing through or over other vegetation. It flowers throughout the whole of the summer.

It is a very vigorous grower making shoots sometimes as much as 6 feet (1.8 m) or more in a single season, but needing support by ties or nails to the wall. With such an amount of growth, it is not surprising that some thinning out of old growth is needed every year or so, otherwise a thicket of tangled stems is formed. Plants can be pruned in early spring, severely if necessary, for it flowers on the current year's growth, or in late summer after flowering.

Jasminum nudiflorum, the yellow winter flowering jasmine, is a deciduous shrub of loose habit growing as much as 10 to 15 feet (3–4.5 m) high, but can easily be kept at half that height by pruning. It is quite hardy in the open but when grown with the shelter of a wall comes into flower earlier and is not so likely to be disfigured after severe frosty weather. It is a first rate plant for giving a bright display during mid winter. As it flowers on growth

Above: *Halimium lasianthum* begins flowering in May (see p. 32).
Below: *Eccremocarpus scaber*, a distinctive semi-woody climber (see p. 30).

Above: *Lonicera × brownii*, a decorative and fairly hardy honeysuckle (see p. 39).
Below: *Itea ilicifolia*, a valuable evergreen shrub (see p.35).

made the previous season, any pruning – such as cutting out old or redundant growth – should be done in spring after the flowering season is finished.

Kerria japonica 'Pleniflora' is a deciduous shrub which is quite hardy and will grow to about 10 feet (2.4 m). Its growth is rather lanky and it needs artificial support; wires or trellis are suitable. Double yellow flowers are borne in profusion from April to June. Kerrias are easily increased by cuttings.

Lathyrus latifolius, the everlasting pea, is a hardy perennial that appreciates a good, rich soil. It blooms during July and August and the flowers vary in colour from purple and pink to white. Train it up wire netting or trellis, and water frequently in dry spells. Propagation is by seed sown in the spring or by root or shoot cuttings taken in April.

Members of the **Lonicera** (honeysuckle) family are valued chiefly for their fragrant flowers; there are both climbers and shrubs amongst the genus, and all like a good loamy soil with plenty of moisture to keep their roots cool. Nearly all prefer semi-shade, where the flowering parts of the plant are in sunlight, conditions similar to those required by the clematis. They require little annual pruning except for an occasional thinning of old or weak growth and tying in all new growth wherever possible.

Several species are well worth including; *Lonicera* × *americana* is an extremely vigorous and free flowering plant, which grows to a height of 18 to 20 feet (5.4–6.2 m). The flowers are fragrant, opening white but gradually ageing to deep yellow with a tinge of purple on the outside of each flower. It is a first-class plant, flowering in June and July.

Lonicera japonica 'Halliana' is a vigorous twiner which is more or less evergreen, and if well grown can make a show during June and July with very fragrant flowers of pure white becoming yellow with maturity.

Our native honeysuckle, *Lonicera periclymenum*, often seen scrambling over the hedgerows in the countryside, is well worth including if space permits. The flowers are fragrant, whitish yellow suffused with purple, produced in close whorls at the end of the twining shoots from June till August and sometimes later. The form 'Serotina' is later in flowering, from July to October, with a similar type of growth and flowers reddish purple outside, creamy white changing to yellow on the inside.

Lonicera sempervirens, the trumpet honeysuckle, is a very beautiful species from the United States, but unfortunately it is a plant which only does really well in milder parts of the country. From June until the autumn its whorls of bright orange-scarlet blossoms are offset well above the glaucous green oval leaves.

In colder gardens where L. *sempervirens* does not grow successfully one can try L. × *brownii*. This is a hybrid between L. *sempervirens* and L. *hirsuta*, a semi-evergreen twiner of moderate growth, producing orange-scarlet flowers during the summer months. It is a good wall plant which has inherited much of the beauty of L. *sempervirens* and the hardiness of L. *hirsuta* (see p.37).

Lonicera tragophylla, a vigorous deciduous honeysuckle from central China, has large flowers, of probably the brightest yellow to be seen in honeysuckles; they are borne in large clusters of ten to twenty during June and July, and contrast well with the oval glaucous green leaves. One great disappointment of this lovely plant is that it has no fragrance. It is perfectly hardy and appears to thrive best in southern England if planted in semi-shade.

No selection would be complete without L. *etrusca*, a very fine Mediterranean species which requires the protection of a south wall if it is to be seen at its best. It has the same type of growth as the common species, but is freer and more vigorous; the very fragrant flowers, yellow, tinged with red, begin to open in July and go on flowering until the autumn on the current season's growth.

The genus **Magnolia** provides some of the most handsome of all flowering trees. Although the majority are perfectly hardy and grow well in the open ground, there are a number well suited for wall cultivation providing the soil is well drained and enriched with plenty of peat and well decayed leafmould, or other forms of compost at the time of planting.

Magnolia denudata – known as the Yulan – was introduced into this country from China in 1788, and has proved to be one of the most beautiful and distinctive of all the magnolias having large, glistening white, well-shaped flowers displayed in early spring. Unfortunately in some seasons the blooms can be damaged by frost, which is the reason why it is often grown in the shelter of a south or west-facing wall.

One of the most popular and widely grown is *Magnolia* × *soulangeana* (which has M. *denudata* as one of its parents and which it closely resembles in its low spreading habit of growth) with flowers varying in different shades of mauve on the outside of the petals (see p. 40).

There are several forms of this hybrid (M. *denudata* and M. *liliiflora*) in cultivation, all varying in colour and shape of flowers, but one of the best with white fragrant flowers is *Magnolia* × *soulangeana* 'Alba Superba'. This is sometimes known as 'Alba', a name also applied to a similar form of M. × *soulangeana*, 'Amabilis'. But one of my favourites is *Magnolia* × *soulangeana* 'Rustica Rubra', another fine form with large globular rosy purple flowers often

Above: *Magnolia × soulangeana*, one of the best known members of this handsome genus (see p. 39).
Below: *Rosa* 'Mme Grégoire Staechelin', a climber flowering in early summer (see p. 47).

Above: *Piptanthus laburnifolius*, an evergreen shrub suitable for a wall (see p. 43).
Below: *Solanum crispum* 'Glasnevin', a vigorous, loose-spreading rambler (see p. 49).

flowering just as the leaves are about to unfold.

Magnolia stellata, a native of Japan, a much branched shrub with a compact habit of growth, makes another useful plant. The highly scented white, star-shaped flowers are freely produced in March and April, but as it flowers so early in the year the delicate flowers are liable to frost damage. For the small garden and wall cultivation this is a most desirable species.

Magnolia grandiflora is probably the most handsome of all the evergreen species in cultivation; it was introduced from the southern United States to this country in the early 18th century, and makes a very fine tree. Many large specimens are to be seen growing in some of the very large private or public gardens, but it does need a lot of space to develop to the full and must be well secured to the wall by strong wires, hooks or other means of support against strong winds.

The leathery large leaves are dark glossy green, covered beneath with thick red brown felt particularly when young, and the very fine creamy white, bowl-shaped flowers are large and fragrant, continually produced during the late summer and autumn. There are named seedling forms in cultivation each of which claim to be better than the type, more compact in growth, or either having larger flowers or some slight variation in leaf shape.

Myrtus communis, the common myrtle, is not hardy enough to grow in the open in most districts, but it does make a neat and pleasing evergreen shrub for covering a wall with its brilliant dark leaves contrasting with the large white rounded flowers, in the centre of which are conspicuous clusters of numerous stamens. The flowers are usually solitary on slender stalks about one inch (2.5 cm) long arising from the leaf axils in July and August.

Osmanthus delavayi. This charming evergreen shrub was introduced from western China in 1890 and is ideal for wall cultivation, because although it is hardy in the open at Kew and other parts of southern England and the west, the flowers are often damaged by late spring frosts. The plant is relatively slow growing with a spreading bushy habit eventually reaching a height of 6 feet (1.8 m) or more. It has small leathery dark green glossy leaves and clusters of small pure white funnel-shaped flowers which are very fragrant. These are produced in the axils of the leaves on growth made the previous season, therefore any pruning required should be done immediately after the flowering season.

Parthenocissus: *Parthenocissus henryana* is hardy and quick growing with attractive dark purplish green, deeply lobed leaves, which are beautifully marked by pink and white midribs and veins. In addition it is self-clinging and the leaves, which have more pronounced markings when the plant is grown in shade, turn shades of red in the autumn. *Parthenocissus tricuspidata*, a species from China, Korea and Japan, is well known for forming a dense cover on old town walls and for its brilliant autumn colour, as well as for its incorrect name of Virginia creeper. The true Virginia creeper is in fact *P. quinquefolia* from eastern U.S.A. Its leaves are usually composed of five oval stalked leaflets which are glaucescent beneath, while those of *P. tricuspidata* are broadly egg-shaped and three lobed. Both are self-clinging, turn colour richly in autumn and are valuable for covering high walls (see p.8).

Few of the passion flowers are suited for growing outdoors except in the more favoured parts of Britain, but I have seen several good specimens of the blue passion flower **Passiflora caerulea** growing successfully in the south on a warm sheltered wall. Given these conditions and a well drained soil, plants will quite often come through a mild winter, although they may suffer during a severe one, which is to be expected being a native of southern Brazil. But for anyone who is prepared to take a risk it can be a most rewarding plant. As a precaution the lower 3 to 4 feet (90–120 cm) of stem should be given some protective covering against possible frosty weather.

It is a vigorous climber which will cover quite a large area of space in a growing season, supporting itself by means of tendrils produced at the ends of the leaves. It does sometimes need extra support, such as the use of strong bamboo stakes and tying material, particularly when young plants are being trained. The flowers are borne freely on long stalks on the current year's growth, and are large pale greenish blue in colour, often 4 inches (10 cm) across, with that remarkable fascinating centre which is characteristic of this well-known flower (see p.44).

Pilostegia viburnoides (often known as *Schizophragma viburnoides*), a Chinese evergreen climber which will grow up to 10 feet (3 m) or more, is another very useful self-clinging plant which climbs by means of aerial roots. The dull green leathery leaves contrast well with the white terminal panicles of flower in late summer, and it is the conspicuous stamens which make the inflorescence so attractive. A good specimen which flowers profusely every year is to be seen at Kew growing on a south wall.

The Himalayan **Piptanthus laburnifolius** (syn. *P. nepalensis*), sometimes called the evergreen laburnum, is a first-class plant for a wall not only because it is an attractive shrub but also because it is not generally hardy. It will reach a height of 6 to 7 feet (1.8–2.1 m) and has strong, upright, green woody shoots. These carry glossy trifoliolate leaves, grey beneath, and in late spring they

Above: *Vitis coignetiae*, a very strong-growing vine with large and ornamental foliage, which turns colour in autumn (see p. 51).
Below: the passion flower, *Passiflora caerulea*, is well worth trying outside (see p.43).

Above: *Wisteria sinensis* is the species widely grown, often reaching a great age (see p. 51).
Below: *Ribes speciosum* bears striking fuchsia-like flowers (see p.46).

carry erect clusters of deep yellow pea-shaped flowers (see p.41).

Prunus triloba ('Multiplex'; 'Plena') is a beautiful Chinese cherry which although hardy can be seen at its best when trained against a south or west wall. It will reach a height of 10 feet (3 m) or more, and flowers in great profusion about the end of March or early April with large pink double blossoms. As the flowers are produced on the shoots of the previous summer, these should be pruned back immediately after flowering to about 2 or 3 inches (5–7 cm) from the old wood, so encouraging strong new growth from dormant basal buds (see p.18).

Pyracantha, the fire-thorn, is a very useful group of evergreen plants, all of which have a profusion of small white flowers in June. They are grown chiefly for the freedom with which they produce their berries in autumn, when they look most attractive if neatly trained against a wall or fence, although they are also hardy in an open situation. They need only occasional pruning to keep them within bounds.

Probably the best known is *P. coccinea*, a south European species with clusters of coral-red fruits. Its cultivar 'Orange Glow' is more widely grown, being more vigorous in growth with larger orange berries, which make a wonderful display. *Pyracantha atalantioides* is equally attractive with dark glossy evergreen foliage and scarlet fruits which usually ripen later and remain on the bush much longer than *P. coccinea*. It too is a very strong grower.

Pyracantha rogersiana is a much less robust grower with small, glossy evergreen leaves and fearsome thorns. It bears an abundance of orange berries which remain fresh until February-March, providing the birds do not take them. The cultivar 'Flava' has very lovely bright yellow fruits. Both plants will do well in positions which get little or no sun during the day.

Ribes speciosum. A very decorative deciduous, or partly ever-green, shrub belonging to the gooseberry family. As it is a native of California it prefers a well drained soil and sheltered sunny position, attaining a height of 5 to 6 feet (1.5–1.8 m) or more in some districts.

The strong spiny shoots and branches are clothed with small glossy roundish leaves not unlike those of a gooseberry, on which hang clusters of bright crimson pendant flowers not unlike tiny fuchsia blooms, which in some seasons produce small bristly red gooseberry-like fruits (see p.45).

Romneya coulteri, native of California, is another attractive plant which thrives against a warm south-facing wall in well drained soil. It is a semi-shrubby perennial with a fleshy rootstock which makes it difficult to transplant once established. It is best treated as a herbaceous perennial, cutting back the woody shoots to within a few inches of the ground each spring. This encourages strong new shoots 4 to 6 feet (1.2–1.8 m) high, bearing glaucous blue grey foliage and producing large white poppy-like flowers with conspicuous golden yellow stamens from June until early autumn. Young plants may take a few years to become established. In colder districts some light winter protection around the base of the plants may be advisable.

Most climbing species of **Rosa** are too vigorous to train on walls but are spectacular when growing up and through trees. On the other hand R. *banksiae*, the Banksian rose, which has been in cultivation for almost 200 years, will grow successfully on a south wall. It is evergreen and thornless, and the growths though slender, will grow many feet in a season. It only flowers once a year in May and June. Usually the flowers are of a soft yellow, single or double, but they may be white; the double form, scented of violets, is more easily obtained. 'Mermaid' is a most beautiful plant for walls with sprays of large pale primrose yellow single flowers which start to open in June and carry on to the autumn frosts. It is semi-evergreen and has glossy bronzy green foliage and vicious spines. It is altogether far more vigorous and hardy than R. *bracteata*, the Macartney rose, which is one of its parents.

Other popular and easily available roses that can be grown up walls successfully include 'Albertine', which has salmon-pink flowers and grows up to 15 feet (4.6 m); 'Golden Showers', with large, golden-yellow blooms, 6–8 ft (1.8–2.4 m); and 'Mme Grégoire Staechelin' which has coral-pink blooms borne from late spring to early summer, 20 ft (6 m). 'Parkdirektor Riggers' is a very free-flowering climber which bears beautiful deep crimson flowers throughout the summer and early autumn and grows to 12–15 feet (3.7–4.6 m) while 'Zéphirine Drouhin' has lovely bright pink, fragrant flowers which also flower throughout the summer, 10–15 feet (3–4.6 m) (see p. 40). (See also the Wisley Handbook *Roses*.)

There are a number of shrubby late-flowering **salvias** which can be considered for wall planting. *Salvia greggii, S. microphylla* (syn. *S. grahamii*) and its variety *neurepia* are all sub-shrubby Mexican species worth trying at the foot of a warm wall for their brilliant scarlet flowers in late autumn. This can also be said of *Salvia coerulea* (also known as *S. ambigens* and *S. guaranitica*) in which the flowers are deep blue, produced on long terminal racemes. It is a first-class plant 4 to 5 feet (1.2–1.5 m) tall with shoots dying back in winter, but not absolutely hardy in all areas. Plants will require either some protection over the roots or to be lifted and stored like dahlias in some frost-proof building (see p.48).

The genus **Schisandra** is a rather unusual and interesting group

Above: the small shrubby salvias do well at the base of a warm wall (see p.47).
Below: *Schizophrgma integrifolium* is closely related to hydrangea.

of shrubby plants, which make long, vigorous, slender twining shoots each year, on which single pendulous, highly-coloured unisexual flowers are borne in considerable numbers in the leaf axils during April and May. The flowers of S. sphenanthera are bright orange, and of S. rubriflora are deep crimson. In both, the red fruits are borne on stalks some four to six inches (10–15 cm) long. Both species will eventually reach a height of 10 to 12 feet (3–3.6 m). They are not very fastidious as to soil requirements, but seem to succeed best on a sheltered wall partially shaded from the midday sun of summer. I have seen them flowering and growing well on a wall facing north and east.

Schizophragma integrifolium, another magnificent Chinese plant, is a strong growing climbing shrub, having large heart-shaped deciduous leaves 4 to 6 inches (10–15 cm) long and the same mode of growth as *Pilostegia viburnoides* (see p. 43) to which it is closely allied.

The fertile inconspicuous flowers are surrounded by remarkable sterile flowers consisting of enormous creamy white bracts sometimes as much as 4 inches (10 cm) long, flowering during July. The plant seems to dislike full sun, particularly in the southern parts of the country.

Where space permits **Solanum** is a worthwhile group of plants, best described as very vigorous ramblers which require some support. First is *Solanum crispum*, introduced from Chile about 1830; when grown at its best it is a most graceful and lovely plant and quite hardy if grown on a south or west wall. It is a very quick grower, more or less evergreen with a loose, spreading habit. On growth made during the current season, the potato-like flowers are produced very freely during June and July, deep lavender in colour with conspicuous yellow stamens in the centre of each flower. The cultivar 'Glasnevin' is the best form to grow on account of its longer season of flower (see p.41).

The other species S. jasminoides, also an evergreen, is slender and twining in growth and slightly more tender, which is not surprising since it is a native of Brazil. However, it will thrive and flower well if given a warm sheltered position and a well drained soil. It flowers from July to September in great profusion, the individual flowers being pale blue in colour and borne in loose clusters on the current season's growth. There is also a white-flowered variety.

Solanums normally flower on long stalked corymbs on growth made during the current year; any pruning required should therefore be done in spring before new growth starts. The pruning consists of cutting out the old flower heads from the previous year and any very old stems or overcrowded growth.

Apart from this no hard pruning is required. Tie in all new vigorous growth as it develops during the summer.

A highly ornamental and attractive shrub is **Sophora tetraptera**, a native of New Zealand, where it is called Kowhai. It makes a large shrub or small tree in this country, with golden yellow, pea-like flowers carried on pendulous racemes during May and early June. Its pinnate leaves give the whole plant a very light and graceful appearance. A plant growing on the west wall of the Temperate House at Kew has come through severe winters unharmed. It produces plenty of seed especially after a good summer.

Stauntonia hexaphylla is a very strong growing climber, with leathery evergreen leaves composed of up to seven leaflets, and fragrant, violet tinted white flowers.

Another evergreen **Trachelospermum jasminoides** (*Rhyncospermum*) is a delightfully shrubby plant with a twining habit of growth, which eventually reaches a height of 6 to 8 feet (1.8–2.4 m), although young plants seem to be slow to make a start. Its pure white, fragrant, jasmine-like flowers are produced in July and August and look very effective against the dark glossy evergreen leaves. It is quite hardy on a south or west wall, and does not need any artificial support.

Virginia creeper (see *Parthenocissus quinquefolia* p. 43).

Vitis, the vine family, includes many species and varieties grown chiefly for their attractive foliage, but also for their fruits. Many are really too vigorous for all but large gardens with ample wall space, but some of those described below can be grown satisfactorily as long as they are restrained (i.e. pruned back and tied regularly).

Vitis 'Brant' is a strong growing hybrid which is sometimes listed under *V. vinifera*, the common grape vine. It has attractive 3 to 5 lobed leaves, which turn to shades of dark red and purple in autumn, and an additional attraction is cylindrical bunches of sweet, aromatic, dark purple grapes with a bloom. Of the common grape vine itself the clone 'Purpurea' has claret-purple leaves which contrast well with silver foliage plants.

Vitis amurensis from Manchuria is moderately strong growing with broad 3 to 5 lobed leaves which colour a wonderful red in autumn.

Vitis coignetiae is exceptionally vigorous with splendid rounded, dark green leaves, which are sometimes as much as 12 inches (30 cm) long and 10 inches (25 cm) broad. Though they often change to various shades of red in the autumn, they give an air of almost tropical luxuriance throughout the growing season. As with most strong growing *Vitis* it is necessary in February or early March of each year to prune back the shoots to 2 or 3 buds at the base of the previous season's growth so as to keep the plant within bounds. Where it is necessary to increase its size to cover more wall space in subsequent years, select a few of the strong growths and prune back to 12 or 18 inches (30–45 cm) in length, or longer if required, of the previous season's growth (see p.44).

Winter sweet (see *Chimonanthus praecox* p. 25).

Wisteria is one of the most ornamental deciduous hardy climbers we have for outdoor cultivation. With long hanging racemes of mauve or lilac flowers, it is too familiar a sight to need description. Wisterias are easily cultivated and will grow in any good soil, but a sunny position is essential to get them to flower well, therefore a wall makes an ideal site.

If planted in a restricted area a fair amount of pruning may have to be done each year to keep them within bounds; usually the long annual shoots not required should be shortened back to about 6 inches (15 cm) long in early August and these shortened shoots cut back again to within three or four buds during the winter. If left unpruned plants are apt to grow into a thick tangle of inter-twining stems, which generally do not flower, for the best sprays are produced from buds formed towards the base of the current season's growth. They can also damage drainpipes and guttering if allowed to get out of control. In young plants, however, a certain amount of this whippy growth must be retained when a young plant is being trained into position. For the first two or three years after planting a young plant may only produce a limited amount of new growth; this is to be expected until a greater root system has been built up, after which the annual growth will increase considerably.

Wisteria sinensis (W. chinensis) is the species commonly grown and many fine old specimens are to be seen, some of which have been grown in this country for well over a hundred years. It is a very vigorous grower and if correctly trained in its young state will cover a large wall space and flower freely in May. Quite often a second but much smaller crop of flowers is produced during August on the current year's growth (see p.45).

There is also a white flowered form 'Alba' which forms an effective contrast when grown with the type.

A less common species is *Wisteria venusta*, which is not such a strong grower. It is similar to *W. sinensis* but the flowers are larger and are a lovely pure white with a yellow tinge at the base of each flower, and delicately fragrant. It comes into bloom after *W. sinensis* has finished.

Above: *Lathyrus odoratus*, the popular annual sweet pea (see p. 55).
Below left: *Rhodochiton volubile*, a Mexican climber which flowers profusely throughout the summer and autumn (see p. 56).
Below right: *Tropaeolum peregrinum*, the canary creeper, easily raised from seed (see p. 57).

Annual climbing plants

There are quite a number of annual climbing plants which can be successfully grown in association with the more permanent plants, particularly on parts of the wall which are not already clothed. They can also be used for filling up other gaps where the stems of some of the taller and stronger growing plants have become bare at the base (the rose 'Mermaid' has this tendency), thus providing a means of support up which the annuals can climb and eventually becoming attached through the upper branches by the time they reach flowering stage.

The extra shelter and protection, particularly along a south or west-facing wall, provide good growing conditions for some of the half-hardy annuals which are often grown in cool greenhouse conditions.

Seed should be sown in a well-drained potting compost or seed compost during April and early May and placed in a little heat (50–55°F, 10–13°C) to hasten germination. If no heat is available plants can be successfully raised using a cold frame, or even cloches.

When the seedlings are large enough prick them out, either singly, or three to a $3\frac{1}{2}$ inch (9 cm) size pot, according to their vigour. Once established the seedlings can be transferred to a cold frame for hardening off, eventually planting them into their flowering position with the least possible root disturbance. A few short twigs, pea sticks or similar material placed around the young plants to give them support can be advantageous at planting time.

Some of the more tender types of annuals should not be sown until the middle of May when growing conditions are warmer and the chances of late frosts have disappeared.

It is possible to sow the hardier types direct into the positions where they are to flower; if this is done care should be taken not to sow too thickly. When the seedlings are large enough to handle, thin out to 3 or 4 inches (7–10 cm) apart, or even more, according to their vigour.

In some of the larger well-stocked garden centres some of these plants can be found already established in pots or containers ready for planting at the appropriate time of the season.

Blumenbachia lateritia. This curious Chilean plant has also been known as *Caiophora laterita* and *Loasa laterita*. The stems have a twining habit of growth, up to 4 to 5 feet (1.2–1.5 m) in height, having divided pinnate or deeply lobed leaves. Single bright orange-red flowers are borne on long twisting stalks which enable the plant to support itself. *Blumenbachia* flowers well into the autumn, and as the long narrow fruits develop they take on a very unusual spiral or twisting effect.

Both the stem and leaves are covered with stinging hairs, making the plant very difficult to handle and necessitating the use of gloves. It is best treated as a half hardy annual, seed being sown singly in pots in spring, preferably in a little heat, and grown on. After hardening off the seedlings should be transferred to their permanent flowering position in early May in a warm sheltered position, allowing 6 to 8 inches (15–20 cm) between each plant.

Canary creeper (see *Tropaeolum peregrinum*, p. 57).

Cardiospermum halicacabum, commonly called the balloon vine or heart-pea, originates from the tropics and is a very interesting rapid-growing, climbing annual up to 6 feet (1.8 m) tall which is able to support itself by tendrils.

The slender, pointed and deeply-toothed light green foliage creates a very feathery appearance from which arise clusters of small white flowers, followed by large green ornamental inflated seed pods containing seeds which have medicinal properties. It is for these attractive fruits that the plant is grown.

Cobaea scandens, also known as the cup and saucer flower, is a native of Central and South America. This strong growing climber will reach a height of 15 feet (4.5 m) or more, and has angular branching stems which bear oval-shaped leaflets, sometimes with tendrils attached; the large bell-shaped solitary flowers are violet on the outside and greenish white on the inside, and are produced in succession from July to October.

Although best suited for a cool greenhouse it will thrive in a warm sheltered position on a south or west-facing wall, but is best treated as an annual and raised each year from seed sown in early spring in a little heat.

Cucumis anguria is a slender climbing annual from the American tropics. When grown on a wall, this plant will reach a height of 6 to 8 feet (1.8–2.4 m) bearing small lobed leaves and solitary flowers from which are produced attractive gooseberry-like gourds during the summer and autumn. *Cucumis* is best raised from seed in early May with the aid of a little heat, similar to the requirements of marrows and cucumbers to which it is closely allied.

Cucurbita pepo is a very variable species which botanically covers a wide variety of ornamental grounds, pumpkins, and marrows of various shapes, sizes and colouring when in fruit (which is the feature for which they are prized). They are very vigorous in growth with large dark green leaves, some palmate, lobed or roundish in shape, and they need support and tying up during the height of its growing season. *Cucurbita* is best raised from seed in late spring, and given the same cultural conditions as the garden marrow, with plenty of water during the dry summer periods.

Humulus japonicus var. **lutescens** is an interesting, vigorous Japanese climber, grown mainly for its large palmate-shaped leaves which are gold or bronze yellow in colour. This species can be grown from seed and treated as an annual, although there is also a variegated form having green-gold leaves which can be just as attractive but does not always come true from seed; the true variegated plant must be raised from cuttings.

Ipomoea purpurea (morning glory), is a very handsome twiner, growing 6 to 8 feet (1.8–2.4 m) in height when grown in the open. It bears cordate-shaped leaves and large exquisite sky-blue flowers from June to September. The flowers are short-lived, being fully open in the morning and closing as the day advances, but the beauty of this plant is that there is always a succession of buds to open during the height of its flowering season.

Lagenaria siceraria (bottle gourd) is from another genus closely allied to *Cucurbita* with similar heart-shaped leaves and tendrils by which it can support its stems. The white, starlike flowers are borne in clusters, and these develop into large, yellow, bottle-shaped fruits. Although usually grown in a warm greenhouse it is hardy enough for cultivation as a summer annual.

Lathyrus odoratus (sweet pea). This very well known and popular annual, noted for its delightful fragrance, makes a useful and easy growing plant, particularly for use on areas of wall where the more permanent plants are still small and have yet to fill their allotted space. It does however need some means of support such as wires, canes or pea sticks to which the tendrils can attach themselves (see p.52).

There are a large number of cultivars and colours available, but I shall not name them here as any good seed catalogue can be consulted for up-to-date varieties.

To get really good quality, sweet peas should be sown in late autumn (September) preferably one or two seeds in a 3½ inch (9 cm) pot or up to 12 seeds in a 6 inch pot (15 cm), in seed or potting compost and overwintered in a cold frame. An alternative is to sow in early spring in similar conditions, or better still with a little heat to hasten germination; harden off before planting out into their flowering position. Growing plants benefit by regular feeding when the buds start to develop.

Maurandya barclaiana, a showy, delicate climber, can climb by the twisting of the leafstalk around any form of support it contacts. This plant often becomes woody at the base and has leaves more or less triangular in shape, toothed and covered with fine downy hairs. The flowers are tubular in shape, not unlike those of a foxglove, usually solitary and produced in the leaf axils. They are violet purple on the outside with a greenish tinge on the inside.

Maurandya erubescens, another species similar in growth and appearance but with rose-pink coloured flowers and whitish tube, is an ideal tender plant for growing outside during the summer months against a sheltered warm south or west facing wall. Sow the seed in early spring in a warm greenhouse, and do not plant outdoors until May or early June when all signs of late frosts have vanished. Both species are now included in the genus *Asarina*.

Nasturtium (see *Tropaeolum major* opposite).

Quamoclit coccinea (star ipomoea). A charming little annual twining herb growing 3 to 4 feet (0.9–1.2 m) and sometimes higher, is ideal for a warm sheltered pocket, and has slender, pointed, sword-like leaves from the axils of which grow tubular-shaped flowers 1 to $1\frac{1}{2}$ inches (2–3 cm) in length, scarlet on the outside with yellow in the throat.

Quamoclit lobata is sometimes known as *Mina lobata* or *Ipomoea versicolor*. Another vigorous twining plant similar in habit to the previous species, it grows to a height of 4 to 5 feet (1.2–1.5 m) and sometimes taller in a hot summer, having small lobed leaves, and clusters of tubular flowers which are bright crimson turning to orange and then yellow with age. It flowers from June to September.

Quamoclit pennata (Cyprus vine) is sometimes grown under the name *Ipomoea quamoclit*, and is another species with similar slender twining habit which grows to the same height as the previous species. It has fine pinnate leaves and scarlet, funnel-shaped flowers from June to September. A variety with white flowers is also known and ocasionally seen in cultivation.

All the species of *Quamoclit* are best treated as half hardy annuals, and can be raised from seed sown in a little heat if available, alternatively they may be sown in the open where they are to flower in May. They are now included in the genus *Ipomoea*.

Rhodochiton volubile, sometimes called *R. atrosanguineum*, is an extremely beautiful and free flowering Mexican climber, which can be successfully grown out of doors if given a warm, sheltered south facing situation, where the stems can twine to effect among other small foliage plants (see p.52).

The leaves are cordate in shape, being somewhat slender and pointed with long twisting leaf stalks which help it to climb. The curious dark blood-red, almost black, parasol-shaped flowers look very effective with the wide saucer shaped rose-pink calyx.

Sow the seed in March or early April preferably in a little heat, and harden off before planting out. It will give a long season of flower starting from June until late autumn.

Sweet pea (see *Lathyrus odoratus* p. 55).

Thunbergia alata (commonly called blackeyed Susan). This plant, a native of South Africa, has become very popular for growing outside during the summer months.

It is a soft hairy twining annual, growing to a height of 5 feet (1.5 m) or more during a hot season, with ovate to cordate-shaped leaves and decorative flowers of rich orange with a distinct blackish-brown centre surrounded by two large inflated bracts. Other coloured forms are in cultivation, varying from white through to shades of yellow.

Trichosanthes anguina (serpent or snake gourd). This is a tall, slender, twining annual with soft, downy stems, roundish leaves, and fragrant clusters of white fringed flowers which develop into very long fruits, sometimes twisted, with green and white stripes when young but turning to a bright orange when ripe. This gourd requires similar conditions to *Cucumis* (p.54).

Tropaeolum peregrinum (*T. aduncum*) is commonly called canary creeper. This is one of the most attractive climbing annuals within the genus (see p.52).

The soft green stems will grow up to 6 to 8 feet (1.8–2.4 m) high, bearing deeply-cut, lobed glaucous green leaves which make a fine contrast to the fringed lemon-yellow spurred flowers, each arranged on long stalks giving a long season of bloom throughout the summer; a most rewarding plant.

Seed should be sown in April and early May, singly in small pots or 3 seeds in a $3\frac{1}{2}$ inch (9 cm) size pot, germinated in a cold frame and planted out to the flowering position when large enough. Seed may also be sown direct into the flowering position in a well drained but not too rich soil.

Requiring similar cultivation is the ever popular garden nasturtium **Tropaeolum majus**, a vigorous annual, which has roundish glabrous green leaves. The large usually orange (although other colours are obtainable) flowers continue throughout the summer months and well into the autumn. The nasturtium is one of the easiest annuals to grow and will flourish on a poor, dry soil. If it is to be treated as a climber some means of support is required, but it can also be left to trail along the ground where it will grow and flower quite successfully.

Above: a plum tree trained against a wall.
Below: peach 'Peregrine' fruits in early August.

Wall-trained fruit

Fruits are another group of plants which enjoy the shelter of a wall if space is available; they include apples, pears, plums (including gages), peaches, apricots and nectarines, and all provide, in addition to good quality fruit, a display of flower in the spring. Apples are the least likely to need the shelter of a wall, but the others benefit from the extra warmth which will improve the flavour of the fruits.

Good examples of trained fruit trees can still occasionally be seen on kitchen garden walls in some of the large private gardens, all beautifully pruned and trained with not a shoot out of place, the results of many years of work from the skilled gardener. Nowadays, with smaller gardens, they are sometimes trained on a suitable house or boundary wall.

Normally all these different types of fruits, with perhaps the exception of peaches, nectarines and apricots, are also successful in the open ground, but growing them on a wall does afford some protection from late spring frosts when the trees are in flower; this particularly applies to plums and gages. It is considered that some of the finest flavoured dessert plums and gages are produced from trees grown against a warm south or west-facing wall.

It is very important to purchase young trees from a reputable fruit grower or a good garden centre, and to make sure that they are healthy and growing on the appropriate rootstock. Work at research stations has produced dwarfing rootstocks which are particularly suitable for using in a small space and these are generally the best choice for growing against a wall. The various methods of training, such as cordon, espalier, or fan (see p. 13) give trees which make maximum use of the space available. They may be purchased as 'maidens' (i.e. one year old plants) by the experienced grower and then pruned and trained in accordance with the form of tree he wishes to grow. These are cheaper to buy and usually grow away better than older trees, but for the beginner it is probably better to buy trees up to three or more years old which have already been shaped by the nurseryman.

Planting can be done at any time between November and March providing the weather is fine and the ground not frozen; make sure that the trees have a good root system with plenty of fibrous roots attached. Many garden centres now have fruit trees established in containers which enable planting to be carried out at more or less any time of the year with the least possible disturbance of the root ball.

In all cases fruit trees that are to be grown against a wall prefer a fertile and well-drained soil that has been well dug and prepared before planting as the trees are to remain in that one position for many years to come; this particularly applies to apples and pears. On poor sandy or acid soil, well decayed manure or compost should be incorporated with the addition of a moderate amount of old mortar rubble or some other form of lime; this is particularly beneficial to plums, gages and other stone fruits.

All fruits require plenty of light and moisture during the growing season, and ample space to grow and develop, so the correct distance between trees should be ascertained before planting. It is also wise to avoid planting too close to large surface rooting trees such as elm and poplar, which can soon become a nuisance and impoverish the soil within the borders adjoining the wall.

Once the young trees have been planted, staking and wiring the wall (see p. 12) will be necessary to keep the tree firmly in position, and for tying in the new growth as it develops.

Where ample wall space is available the common fig (*Ficus carica*) is worth growing, chiefly for its fruit, although its handsome ornamental foliage is also most attractive during the summer months. Figs require plenty of sun and warmth and therefore prefer a south-facing wall. It is generally accepted that ripe fruits are more often obtained from trees which are grown in the warmer areas such as the south and west of England, conditions further north of the country being generally too cold for success. One of the most popular and reliable varieties to grow is 'Brown Turkey'.

Figs are generally fan trained (see p. 13) to obtain the best results, tying in new healthy growth when necessary during the growing season. The roots should be confined to a restricted area in order to encourage fruit production, so the fig can be grown in a narrow border.

Winter pruning consists mainly of cutting out all diseased or frost damaged wood and other weak growth which crosses the main branches; this should be done during late March when the severe winter weather has passed.

For further detailed information on cultural instructions and requirements regarding the growing and training of fruit trees on walls, see the well illustrated and comprehensive book entitled *The Fruit Garden Displayed* published by Cassell for the Royal Horticultural Society.

SOME RECOMMENDED VARIETIES:

Apples

Dessert (eating)

Beauty of Bath (August)
Egremont Russet (October–November)
Epicure (August–September)
James Grieve (September–October)
Laxton's Fortune (September–October)
Ellison's Orange (September–November)
Sunset (November–December)
Cox's Orange Pippin (November–January)
Tydeman's Late Orange (April–February)

Pears

Dessert

Williams Bon Chrétien (September)
Louise Bonne of Jersey (October)
Beurré Superfin (October)
Beurré Hardy (October)
Doyenné du Comice (November)
Conference (October–November)

Plums

Dessert and culinary

Victoria (mid August)
Pershore (late August)
Warwickshire Drooper (September)
Marjorie's Seedling (September)

Gages

Dessert

Cambridge Gage (end of August)
Denniston's Superb (mid August)
Oullins Golden Gage (mid August)
Jefferson (early September)

Apricots

Moorpark (August)

Nectarines

John Rivers (mid July)
Lord Napier (early August)
Humboldt (mid August)
Pine Apple (early September)

Peaches

Hale's Early (July)
Peregrine (early August)
Rochester (early August)
Royal George (end of August)
Bellegarde (early to mid September)

Cherries

Most sweet cherries grow too vigorously to be trained to a limited space on a back garden wall. There is not yet a dwarfing rootstock for cherries which would control their growth. Another difficulty with cherries is that at least two different cultivars need to be planted together to get pollination and fruiting. These two problems can be partially overcome by planting a tree of the self-fertile variety 'Stella' on the rootstock 'Colt', which is semi-dwarfing.

Acid cherries, e.g. 'Morello', are suitable for walls as they are self-fertile and relatively small trees which can be easily trained, usually in the fan-form.

Grapes

Vines can also be grown against walls and are very amenable to training. The usual form, however, is a vertical cordon with one or more branches spaced at $3\frac{1}{2}$ to 4 feet (1.2 m) apart, so allowing space for the fruiting lateral shoots. Among suitable cultivars are:

White

Perle de Czaba (late September)
New York Muscat (mid to end October)
Chasselas (late October)

Black

Noir Hatif de Marseilles (late September)
Cascade (Seibel 13.053) (early October)
Muscat Bleu (mid-October)

(See also the Wisley Handbook, *Grapes Indoors and Out*.)

Soft fruit

Red and white currants and gooseberries can also be grown against walls, with one, two or even three vertical "arms".

Plants suitable for various aspects

Most wall plants, with the exception of a few that prefer shade and cooler growing conditions, succeed equally well on a wall facing between east, south and west. For preference I would choose a south wall, for it is there that the plants get the benefit of the maximum amount of sunshine. Some prefer a more westerly aspect to get the benefit from the hottest part of the day which can quite often be in the early afternoon during the summer. For plants that bloom in early spring, an east facing wall is less satisfactory. Many flowers will survive a few degrees of frost without injury provided they can thaw out slowly, but if a late frost is followed by bright early morning sunshine, the same flowers receiving a quick thaw can be spoilt. For these plants it may be advantageous to plant them on a south-west to west facing wall. There are, however, many plants that will thrive on walls exposed to the east and south-east, although some discretion may be used in selecting those plants that bloom after March or early April which would miss the late spring frosts. Walls facing north are least satisfactory of all and comparatively few climbers or shrubs prefer them; it is generally evergreens that do best. Even so some shelter from north and north-east winds by other vegetation or buildings is advantageous. For walls fully exposed to these winds especially in cold districts it is difficult to find interesting plants.

A SELECTION FOR NORTH AND EAST WALLS

Camellia japonica cultivars*
Celastrus orbiculatus
Chaenomeles
Clematis × jackmanii cultivars
Cotoneaster
Euonymus fortunei
Forsythia
Hedera helix and cultivars
Holboellia coriacea
Hydrangea petiolaris
Jasminium officinale
Lonicera tragophylla
Parthenocissus henryana
Parthenocissus quinquefolia
Pyracantha
Schisandra
Schizophragma integrifolia

Most if not all of those items which are listed on a north and east wall will grow also on a south or west wall.

* Except in Scotland and the north of England.

A SELECTION FOR A WEST WALL

Abelia floribunda
Actinidia kolomikta
Camellia sasanqua
Camellia saluenensis
Camellia × *williamsii* cultivars
Ceanothus
Chaenomeles
Chimonanthus praecox
Choisya ternata
Clematis × *jackmanii* cultivars
Cytisus battandieri
Escallonia
Hoheria lyallii
Jasminum nudiflorum
Lonicera
Magnolia denudata
Osmanthus delavayi
Passiflora caerulea
Pilostegia viburnoides
Prunus triloba
Rosa
Solanum crispum
Solanum jasminoides 'Album'
Wisteria sinensis

A SELECTION FOR A SOUTH WALL

Abelia floribunda
Abutilon megapotamicum
Camellia sasanqua
Camellia saluenensis
Camellia × *williamsii* cultivars
Campsis
Ceanothus
Chaenomeles
Choisya ternata
Cistus
Clematis
Cytisus battandieri
Desfontainea spinosa
Escallonia
Lonicera japonica 'Halliana'
Magnolia denudata
Osmanthus delavayi
Prunus triloba
Passiflora caerulea
Pilostegia viburnoides
Solanum crispum
Sophora tetraptera
Teucrium fruticans
Wisteria sinensis

Desfontainea spinosa appreciates the shelter of a wall (see p.30).